10 Seconds:

Success Journal

Do you have an unrealized dream?

What's holding you back?

Tim Marvel

10SecondsDaily.com

**Revolutionize Your Reality
In 10 Seconds a Day**

Books by Tim Marvel:

10 Seconds: An Exercise in Attitude
The Complete Series

10 Seconds: An Exercise in Attitude
Part One: Plant the Seed

10 Seconds: An Exercise in Attitude
Part Two: Work Your Field

10 Seconds: An Exercise in Attitude
Part Three: Share Your Harvest

10 Seconds Success: An Exercise in Career

10 Seconds Pay it Forward: An Exercise in Selflessness

10 Seconds: Success Journal

10 Seconds: Success Journal

by Tim Marvel

Editor: Lori Freeland

Cover Design: Mai Koua

© 2017 Tim Marvel. All rights reserved. No part of the publication may be reproduced, distributed, or transmitted in any form or by any means, including photocopying, recording, or other electronic or mechanical methods, without the prior written permission of the publisher, except in the case of brief quotations embodied in critical reviews and certain other noncommercial uses permitted by copyright law.

To Rockie -
Dreams do come true.

And to all the coaches over the years who have taught me that commitment and effort over time will result in success. Success isn't always about winning the race.
It's about making progress.

Acknowledgments

Journals take many forms. My first journal was introduced to me by Ted Noffsinger, my junior/senior high track coach. He provided a mileage log to each of the runners on his team. By keeping a daily log, I was able to see my efforts pay off on paper. I learned small steps taken in small daily disciplines could lead to great success. By journaling and reviewing my efforts, I made measurable improvements over time.

Coach, thank you for instilling in me a discipline that continues to drive my success all these years later.

Introduction

*Journaling is about documenting your journey.
Success is only a bi-product.*

When you think of a journal what comes to mind? A diary? A to-do list? A planner? Whether you see journaling as a way to remember important past events, a checklist, or a great place to keep track of your goals, it carries the potential to move you forward.

What if, with a little time and effort, you could use your entries to influence personal change? The best part is journaling can be directed toward every part of your life.

One of the biggest questions I hear is why spend time *writing* things when I could be *doing* things? My response is that we make thousands of choices every day that impact the outcome of our lives. We cannot possibly remember how each small decision impacts the results of our effort. By making notes, we give ourselves a powerful tool of proof.

Time for a self-check:
1. What did you accomplish yesterday?
2. What did you accomplish last week?
3. What did you accomplish last month?
4. What did you accomplish last year?

Was it easy to remember yesterday? How about last year? If you struggled, journaling could be a great tool for you. It could also be a starting point for a goal or activity. I like to put a completion dates next to my goals. This allows me to hold myself more accountable for reaching the desired outcome. There is far less of a chance I will make excuses for not making progress if I give myself a deadline and map out a plan to reach it.

Journaling also allows me to track progress. When I first begin to implement change, progress is often difficult to see. But if I've documented my journey, I can go back to a defined time and review the tiny blocks that built my strong foundation.

Journaling reminds me of blogging. Many people read my 200-250 word daily post. Most would be surprised to realize I've blogged more than 250,000 words over the past few years—five minutes at a time. It's not one post that's amazing, but the thousands of words that make a statement about where I was and where I'm going. Just like it's not one journal entry that will outline your success, but the consistency over time that will be your map.

Journaling our tiny steps each day helps process our wins and losses and allows us to learn how to gain better results from our actions. We become more effective and efficient with our effort and learn how to prioritize our time.

Many of my friends use a "To-Done" list. They don't want the pressure of completing their list each day to lead to failure. They document items as they complete them so there's never a loss, but always a win.

They get a sense of accomplishment by adding items to their list. Each day they start with a blank page. Not my favorite, but any process is better than no process at all.

However you choose to journal, remember to stay focused and engaged in the big picture. I'm excited for you to join me on this journey and realize all you can accomplish.

Instructions

Here are a few suggestions to get the most out of this journal.

Step One
- Use the first pages to detail your BIG goal. Be specific.
- Make the goal so big it *scares* you.
- Commit to the goal.
- Add a completion date.
- Take the time to document the goal properly. This could take weeks.

Step Two
- This book contains lined pages for documentation.
- Each page has 20 lines.
- Take as many lines as you need per day.
- Make daily entries about your big goal.
- Keep track of your thoughts.
- Write down one action you took or plan to take.

Now for the fun part. Review your progress on a regular basis. Even though it may not seem like anything's happening daily, when you look back over 30, 60, and 90 days, you'll see what's called the compound effect. It will blow your mind. Especially when you review at the end of the year and see how far you've come from Day One. If you follow these simple daily disciplines, I'm confident you'll see amazing results.

My Goal

To show you how this journal works, let me share one of my biggest goals. As a consultant in the automotive industry, I've had the opportunity to facilitate groups of 250 managers and owners in one-day workshops and loved doing it. But I wanted to move that role outside my industry. To make that happen, I came up with a six-year plan to become a successful author, speaker, and coach.

It was a huge leap to go out on my own so I chose to look at filling my new role like the old story about eating an elephant. How do you eat an elephant? One bite at a time. My initial plan was simple. If I could write one book a year, blog daily, and create and publish 100 videos a year for six years, I felt I would be ready.

Your Goal

What is your BIG GOAL? Maybe in your mind it's not a goal, but a dream. Whatever you're calling it, take time to think it through. It's the most important aspect of the exercise. Remember, BIG GOALS are often made up of smaller goals. When you're ready, use the lines below to describe what you want to come next for you.

_____
_____
_____
_____
_____
_____
_____
_____
_____
_____
_____
_____
_____
_____
_____
_____
_____
_____
_____
_____

My Plan

I'm going to be asking you these same four questions. But first, here's how I answered them when I set out to reach my big goal.

Question #1 Where am I now?
I'd begun blogging two years earlier, but hadn't written a book or made a video.

Question #2 Where do I want to be?
I want to change professions and become a successful trainer, consultant, and author and publish 6 books, 600 videos, and a continuous blog within 6 years.

Question #3 What am I willing to do to get there?
I'll need education. I'll map out learning and seek out people who are doing what I want to do. I'll work on writing my first book daily, attend classes in the evening and weekends, build a website designed to create passive income, and listen to successful speakers. I'll join two speakers' associations and invest time and money in the career I want.

Question #4 Who else knows about my plan?
Everyone. I talk about it every day. My wife is on-board. I can't do this without her. I need her and my friends to hold me accountable by asking how my plan to achieve my goal is going.

What happened after I named my goal and wrote that plan? Within two years, I'd written 5 books, made 400 hundred videos, and created a blog that has been read by over 100,000 people.

Your Plan

It's your turn to fill in the blanks and begin to put your plan into action. You may not have all the answers when you start. I challenge you to keep moving forward with the faith that you're headed the right direction.

Go back and read your big goal, then fill in the following four questions with a concrete plan to make that goal happen. I believe in you.

1. *Where am I right now?* This is your baseline to measure change.

2. *Where do I want to be* in the next month, year, 5 years? These are your short term and long term goals.

3. *What steps are you willing to take to reach those goals?* This is your plan of action.

___

4. *Who knows about your desire to change?* It's difficult to police yourself. This is your accountability.

The Daily Journal

Now that you've written your goal, outlined a plan, and committed to your success, it's time to see what journaling can do for you.

Use the lines that make up this journal to date and write an entry. Watch how each entry moves you closer to your BIG GOAL. By consistently spending a small amount of time focusing on what you want to accomplish, you'll stay engaged in the process that will ultimately lead you where you want to go.

Below is an example of what my journal might look like and how I know at a glance what is not complete. You may want to cross items off the list. As for me, I like to review what I've completed. If I cross through the item, I may not be able to read it.

-    A Dash represents something not completed.
- *   A star represents a completed item.

16 Jan 2017

- Status report (not completed)

* Set flight for Tampa Trip (completed)

* Call Rojelia (completed)

- Schedule Mastermind Group (Not completed)

* Make a list of classes to complete (not complete)

I hope by seeing progress you are excited about your next goal. Your success depends on your daily effort. Avoid asking "why" questions, they only point you toward the past. You can't change what's already happened. Instead, look forward. Ask "what" questions about the future. My hope is that this journal gives you the desire to move farther than you ever imagined.

My Success Journal
Change Starts Here

10 Seconds   A Daily Exercise

10 SecondsA Daily Exercise

10 Seconds — A Daily Exercise

10 Seconds   A Daily Exercise

10 Seconds   A Daily Exercise

10 Seconds

A Daily Exercise

10 Seconds   A Daily Exercise

10 Seconds — A Daily Exercise

10 Seconds — A Daily Exercise

10 Seconds   A Daily Exercise

10 Seconds   A Daily Exercise

10 Seconds — A Daily Exercise

10 Seconds   A Daily Exercise

10 Seconds

A Daily Exercise

10 Seconds

A Daily Exercise

10 Seconds   A Daily Exercise

10 Seconds
A Daily Exercise

10 Seconds A Daily Exercise

10 Seconds   A Daily Exercise

10 Seconds

A Daily Exercise

10 Seconds   A Daily Exercise

10 Seconds — A Daily Exercise

10 Seconds   A Daily Exercise

10 Seconds   A Daily Exercise

10 Seconds

A Daily Exercise

10 Seconds | A Daily Exercise

10 Seconds   A Daily Exercise

10 Seconds   A Daily Exercise

10 Seconds   A Daily Exercise

10 Seconds   A Daily Exercise

10 Seconds A Daily Exercise

10 Seconds   A Daily Exercise

10 Seconds					A Daily Exercise

10 Seconds — A Daily Exercise

10 Seconds

A Daily Exercise

10 Seconds — A Daily Exercise

10 Seconds

A Daily Exercise

10 Seconds — A Daily Exercise

10 Seconds   A Daily Exercise

10 Seconds   A Daily Exercise

10 Seconds — A Daily Exercise

10 Seconds   A Daily Exercise

10 Seconds
A Daily Exercise

10 Seconds

A Daily Exercise

10 Seconds　　　　　　　　　　　　　　　A Daily Exercise

10 Seconds   A Daily Exercise

10 Seconds   A Daily Exercise

10 Seconds   A Daily Exercise

10 Seconds   A Daily Exercise

10 Seconds　　　　　　　　　　　　　　　　　　A Daily Exercise

10 Seconds   A Daily Exercise

10 Seconds A Daily Exercise

10 Seconds   A Daily Exercise

10 Seconds

A Daily Exercise

10 Seconds

A Daily Exercise

10 Seconds

A Daily Exercise

10 Seconds   A Daily Exercise

10 Seconds   A Daily Exercise

10 Seconds   A Daily Exercise

10 Seconds — A Daily Exercise

10 Seconds	A Daily Exercise

10 Seconds   A Daily Exercise

10 Seconds A Daily Exercise

10 Seconds

A Daily Exercise

10 Seconds

A Daily Exercise

10 Seconds　　　　　　　　　　　　　　　　　　A Daily Exercise

10 Seconds   A Daily Exercise

10 Seconds — A Daily Exercise

10 Seconds

A Daily Exercise

10 Seconds

A Daily Exercise

10 Seconds

A Daily Exercise

10 Seconds

A Daily Exercise

10 Seconds   A Daily Exercise

10 Seconds   A Daily Exercise

10 Seconds

A Daily Exercise

10 Seconds

A Daily Exercise

10 Seconds

A Daily Exercise

10 Seconds — A Daily Exercise

10 Seconds   A Daily Exercise

10 Seconds

A Daily Exercise

10 Seconds   A Daily Exercise

10 Seconds

A Daily Exercise

10 Seconds   A Daily Exercise

10 Seconds

A Daily Exercise

10 Seconds   A Daily Exercise

10 Seconds

A Daily Exercise

10 Seconds   A Daily Exercise

10 Seconds   A Daily Exercise

10 Seconds
A Daily Exercise

10 Seconds

A Daily Exercise

10 Seconds

A Daily Exercise

10 Seconds

A Daily Exercise

10 Seconds

A Daily Exercise

10 Seconds — A Daily Exercise

10 Seconds   A Daily Exercise

10 Seconds   A Daily Exercise

10 Seconds   A Daily Exercise

10 Seconds   A Daily Exercise

10 Seconds   A Daily Exercise

10 Seconds										A Daily Exercise

10 Seconds

A Daily Exercise

10 Seconds — A Daily Exercise

10 Seconds　　　　　　　　　　　　　　　A Daily Exercise

10 Seconds — A Daily Exercise

10 Seconds

A Daily Exercise

10 Seconds — A Daily Exercise

10 Seconds   A Daily Exercise

10 Seconds
A Daily Exercise

10 Seconds　　　　　　　　　　　　　　　A Daily Exercise

10 Seconds										A Daily Exercise

10 Seconds

A Daily Exercise

10 Seconds

A Daily Exercise

10 Seconds   A Daily Exercise

10 Seconds	A Daily Exercise

10 Seconds

A Daily Exercise

10 Seconds   A Daily Exercise

10 Seconds

A Daily Exercise

10 Seconds — A Daily Exercise

10 Seconds — A Daily Exercise

10 Seconds   A Daily Exercise

10 Seconds — A Daily Exercise

10 Seconds   A Daily Exercise

10 Seconds — A Daily Exercise

10 Seconds									A Daily Exercise

10 Seconds

A Daily Exercise

10 Seconds   A Daily Exercise

10 Seconds

A Daily Exercise

10 Seconds — A Daily Exercise

10 Seconds — A Daily Exercise

10 Seconds   A Daily Exercise

10 Seconds

A Daily Exercise

10 Seconds   A Daily Exercise

10 Seconds   A Daily Exercise

10 Seconds
A Daily Exercise

Do you struggle with your attitude?

10 Seconds: An Exercise in Attitude

Available now.

Are you tired of feeling defeated before you even start your day?

Between the headlines, social media, and the people around us, we have the potential to be filled with negative input from the moment we wake up to the moment we go to bed. Even while we sleep, we continue to process what we've absorbed.

We become what we believe.

If we live in constant negativity, it's no wonder we struggle to be positive. We may not be able to fix all our problems, but we can change the way we respond.

Our attitude influences our perception. Our perception becomes our reality.

What would happen if we took ten seconds to plant a positive seed in our attitude each morning? Over time, those tiny seeds can shift our perception and help us cultivate a new reality.

Self-reflection is the front line for change.

Feeling stuck in your career?
10 Seconds Success: An Exercise in Career
Available now.

Whether your obstacle is disorganization, lack of confidence, fear of failure, or being overwhelmed with the idea of change, you can move forward. The key to being successful in the future is to learn to be successful where you are right now. Your state of mind matters. *10 Second Success* helps you refocus your attitude and begin to move toward reaching your short and long term goals. Stop standing still.

All you need to get started is one first step.
Take back your life in *10 Seconds* a day.

Meeting goals isn't about grand leaps.
It's about persistent steps and tiny tweaks.

Commit to continue
"The 10 Second Challenge."
Your next ten seconds begin now.
How far will you go?

Visit 10SecondsDaily.com
for additional resources including
daily blogs, videos, workbooks, events,
and to invite Tim to speak at your

organization.